Suddenly

notionpress.com

Suddenly

Astha Pareek

notionpress.com

Notion Press

Old No. 38, New No. 6
McNichols Road, Chetpet
Chennai - 600 031
First Published by Notion Press 2016

ISBN 978-93-5206-689-6

To the Dreams of a Young Girl

Contents

Foreword *xi*

Acknowledgments *xiii*

From Parents *xv*

1. The Ultimate Party Song 3
2. Suddenly 5
3. Trapped in a Paradox 6
4. This is Home 9
5. Are We Any Good? 10
6. Discomfort, Is It? 11
7. Now I know 12
8. When the Coffee is Still Hot 13
9. Audacity of Hope 14
10. Perspective 16
11. Long Way from Home 17
12. Let Us Meet! 18
13. Where Do You Run 20
14. Sweet Little Day 21
15. Pictures 23
16. What are We as a Nation? 25
17. Welcome to Life 27
18. Reach for the Stars 28
19. I Asked for You 30
20. And Life Began 31

21. Little Love 33
22. Changing Paradigm 35
23. Deep in the Corner of My Ashtray 36
24. Let's 38
25. Hypno 40
26. Living in the Head! 41
27. A Breathing Pause 42
28. Tranquil Trail 43
29. Noises in My Head 44
30. Story of a Hope 47
31. Night's Fury 49
32. Once Again 51
33. Questions 52
34. I Shall Call for You 53
35. And I Said to Myself 54
36. The Psychology of Truth 56
37. On the Median of Life 57
38. You Find Me! 59
39. Merely Alive 60
40. World of My Own Making 62
41. A Dedication to Late Mrs Kalpana Chawla 63
42. Look! Where We Have Come? 65
43. My Ignorance Seeks Intellect... 66
44. Give Me Sometime 67
45. Time is Nobody 69
46. Hypnos Song 72
47. It's from You 73
48. You 75

49. Dream 77
50. Life is a Bliss 79
51. When You are Gone 81
52. Immortal Dreams 83
53. Forget Me Not 84
54. I Have to Love Nature 85
55. Trophies of Life 86
56. Life's Brief Grief 87
57. Leaving Behind 88
58. In the Vicinity of Hope 90
59. The Road to Time 92
60. I Am Nowhere 93
61. Adamant in Their Speech 94
62. The Incarnation of Truth 96
63. Parody of Life 97
64. In Me You Flow 99
65. A Dream… I am Living 100
66. Somewhat? 104
67. Only for You 106
68. Plight of the Earliest Bird 108
69. My Mother's Ways 109
70. Celebrated Knights 110
71. The Murli Tales 111
72. Call for Peace 112
73. Mazes 113
74. Once Again-1 114
75. Once Again-2 116
76. Those Little Things 117

77. I Have a Song 118
78. Look Deep Before You Die 120
79. Heal Me 121
80. Should I Thank You? 123
81. Beautiful Night? 124
82. The Wrong World 125
83. Make Me Fly 127
84. Have a 'Fall' 128
85. O What Light 129
86. Garden of Hope 130
87. In the End 131

Foreword

Poetry is one way of looking around, of finding one's world, of exploring relationships, of talking to the world.

Astha was a young girl who took to poetry to do all these things with much enthusiasm, putting in words her personal and social reality. The words, which in many poems rhyme with each other, are drenched in a zest for life and love. They are honest and transparent even if, sometimes, they are unsure. Poetry, all too often, is written not only with words but also with sincerity.

There is an exuberant adolescence – a youthful apprehension of what is happening in the dark interiors of the heart, as well as in the over-lighted exteriors. Astha's poetry does not attempt any concealment: it is an open house full of intensities and anxieties but is also full of hope, expectation and assurance. And yet there are moments of despair:

And hence the humble retreat to despair,
It settles for a holy cause.
Where no true horizon shall declare.
And life runs on a breathing pause.

From bliss to emptiness, with 'breathing silence' roaring unheard, from 'courtyard of life' to 'a tiny garden hope'…the young poet covers a vast complexity of emotions and occasions.

It is tragic that her life was cut short. However, her poetry survives and assures you that it was a life worth living, loving and putting in words.

Ashok Vajpeyi

Hindi Poet, Essayist, Literary-Cultural Critic

Former Chairman, Lalit Kala Akademi (India's National Academy of Arts)

Acknowledgments

Dr. Anju Dhadda Mishra for editing

From Parents

These poems were written by a young girl who is no more in this world. She started to write from a very young age before her teen years while coming in school bus, sometimes writing on a piece of newspaper, school copy, register or diary, and was writing until 5 days before she died in an accident on 12th March 2014, before that she wrote the poem on which the book is also titled "SUDDENLY" on 5th March 2014 which she sang, composed and put on the Youtube and Soundcloud on the same day and asking us to comment. If you read and hear this song you can understand the premonition she had about what FATE had decided though no one can think of the unthinkable at that point of time. In these poems are the dreams, conflicts, life, death, hopes, apprehensions and aspirations of a young girl with a philosophy of her own life.

Her last poem was written on 7th March 2014.

You can contact us to share your reviews and memory on the following addresses:

Dr. S S Pareek
Lecturer's Colony,
City Road near Krishna Art Center
Kishangarh, Rajasthan - 305801
India
Facebook Id: ShyamPareek
Twitter Id: Dr. S S Pareek
Google+ Id: drshyampareek
Email Address:drsspareek@gmail.com
Contact Number: +91-9829159296
Dr. Alka Pareek
Mob.no. +91-9928073786
Email Id : alka.pareek62@gmail.com

It is difficult to think what Astha as a writer would like to say in this regard but her "Welcome" posted in her blog is sufficient to convey what she wanted to share:

Welcome

February 19, 2011

Hi folks,

Although this was never my intention but yes, now I feel like sharing myself, my views (no matter how irrational and immature they might sound!) with the world. So here goes my poems… for the world to stand and praise the almighty for creating a creature like me, who looks introvert but when explored, has huge amounts of trash to empty into this world ☺.

Hope you enjoy this piece of raw junk calamity posted on the web...

Yours forcefully ☺
Astha

Astha Pareek

(1990–2014)

THE ULTIMATE PARTY SONG

March 7, 2014

That's sunshine sparkling haughty
It's on the move, it's naughty
It ain't no fun, just watch in a party
Jump a beat and dance hearty.

You got to let go, set it free
Join the rhythm, the chemistry
Love is the drug, love is the pain
Love is all you got to gain.

Wo oh oh oh ooohooo…
You never know what you're looking at
Maybe some peace maybe some roar
After the song, just get right back to
Whatever you longed for before…
…and some more…
La la lala
La la la la la-2
Can't contain what is inside
It's got a bomb and you got to hide
The last I saw you were running for life
Dance it away, it's not suicide.
You never know what you're looking at

Maybe some peace, maybe some roar
After the song just get right back at
Whatever you longed for before…
…and some more, and more, and more, more…

SUDDENLY

March 5, 2014

Suddenly by the road I see one of me
I don't know if that's true
I wave, I pull back, I just stand still
Like, I don't know it is who.
Though it's far away that I've come
Why am I on the same crossroad?
Oh! In what seems like ages 'n' ages
Have I not grown old?
Knock me out
Pull me in
Make me one of you
Miracle of time, run
Run away with me...
Knock me out
Pull me in
Make me one of you
Miracle of time, run
Run away with me
Run away, oh! You!

TRAPPED IN A PARADOX

January 29, 2014

I'm trapped in me
To be or not to be
It's a fine line
Asundering my sensitivity
One being me
And the other being me
I know not
Who I am
Or who I used to be
I'm trapped in a paradox
A paradox of truth
It changes with time
It changes with itself
Yet it remains a constant
A constant paradox
Of me versus me.
I grab myself
And I let myself go
And yet I see myself go
With the one gone.
It's all a trap.
All of it.
I plan it

I execute it
And then I live it
Every moment being me
...like a time warp over suffocated breaths
I live...
Like a paradox
Defying myself
To myself
Deriving myself
Of myself
Dividing myself
From myself.
I cry
And then I laugh
Though in subtle eerie corners only.
I sympathize
And then I pinch
With a smirk of integrity.
I have found my true victim
Myself.
I play with my prey
And each time I realize
That it's none other than me
The master, the slave, the creator, the destroyer.
I'm scared
And then I gain courage
For I am the terrorist.
I'm aware

And then I lose consciousness
For I have the other role to play
The one of the victim.
I am no more afraid
And then that thought scares me
I have entered a vicious cycle
Of delusional identity
I escape from one to enter another
And when I get tired of both
I sympathize
I cry
I smirk
I pinch
And the cycle continues…

THIS IS HOME

December 25, 2013

Seeking why you lost your way home
Buy yourself a time of peace
Clear those tired, weary glasses
See what made them blurry…
Look in all, look outside
What you find, what you decide
Is your home, always
It's where you belong, always
Take that light
Make it true
Hold a hand
Make it two.
When you cease to belong
It's the heart that's pumping on
And make you believe, always.
This is home, always
This is where you belong, always…

ARE WE ANY GOOD?

November 29, 2013

How good are we
At keeping our eyes closed
At this tongue-twisted rope!
How good are we
For never taking a note
For over-rating that hope.
Oh just how bizarre
Is our world
We crave for acceptance
But seldom brave an act, a word.
Just how good are we
For we know our limit, it's not too far.
It's in our hearts, etched with fear.
It's in our minds, buffed clear.
Are we any good here?
They look us in the eyes
Nothing!
They cry out their hearts and minds
Nothing!
They bed and feed and get burnt out
Nothing!
Oh how good we are
At nothing!

DISCOMFORT, IS IT?

October 3, 2013

Cosmic loss of discomfort,
Of anything that feels like pain.
Everything happens for a reason;
Every reason being gain!
Like the need to be good,
Be good, to be bad again.
Buying goodness each Sunday
In the local charity drain.
Cosmic loss of discomfort,
At every unscathed stain.
Tainting one's own house
Is their only refrain.
Like the need to overlook
Every destitute's bargain.
In exchange for a blessing
They'll take home some grain.

NOW I KNOW

May 17, 2013

Now I know what they mean,
Keep eyes open and still dream…
What is it to fly
Keeping vigil across an endless sky.
Birds flapping wings so fast,
For they know it won't last.
It is an everyday regime,
Now I know what they mean.

WHEN THE COFFEE IS STILL HOT

September 27, 2013

When the coffee is still hot
And the rain still pouring,
The warmth of your eyes
Gazing, adoring.
I turn beauty,
I turn gold.
I see what you do there,
I hear what you've not told.
When the coffee is still hot.
The sweet rising aroma
Ever deluding
In the wisp of smoke
Your breath, bemusing.
I fancy a smile.
I fancy a hold.
In the warmth of your hands
I never was so cold.
While the coffee was still hot.

AUDACITY OF HOPE

May 13, 2013

Audacity of hope,
Aloud;
Not allowed.
Clarity to doubt
Sought;
Not sort.
For keeping what's lost
Discreet;
Discrete.
Whenever we shall meet,
In a loop;
Elope.
Audacity of hope.

Perspective

May 4, 2013

Peering through my lens,
I see beauty dressed in common sense.
Bare, sensitive,
Every single adjective;
Sharing perspective.
You and your neighbours
Behind the walls inseparable.
Open curtains cooperative,
For windows find motive;
Sharing perspective.
Far-off lands, identical aspiration.
Good food, health and lifelong vacation.
Reach that distant relative,
Ring a bell when plaintive.
Sharing perspective!

LONG WAY FROM HOME

March 25, 2013

I've come a long way from home.
The wind, the roads, the water
Brushing my soul – novelty
Lands in ups-and-downs
Skies in brevity.
I've come a long way from home
To make one my own
On my way, away!
People with random faces
Facing the random city
Some happy, some just okay
Some quite fascinating!
I've come a long way from home
And to make one, my own
On my way, away!
Away from home.

LET US MEET!

March 1, 2013

Hey, let us meet on a lousy day
Under a cloudy sky
And let us sway!
Let's make faces
Of white and grey
Clouds in array.
And the dark ones, let them pour
Let's leave traces of our childhood play
As we walk away
And let us catch up, after all, another day
Have you heard that He bends the clay
As He mends the day
Let us pray!
Let's make peace in our hearts and delight
In each compromise
To fill each moment with love
Wipe off heaps of distant fight,
As in supplication we offer
Each waking up to a dove.
Hey, let us meet on a lousy day
Under a cloudy sky

And let us sway!
For all we know, we are here to stay
And a peer to care
Let us play!

WHERE DO YOU RUN

January 3, 2013

What do you run away from?
What do you run away to?
Here is where they all come,
Here is where they all glue.
Do you not see, they find you,
Bind you, run behind you.
Do you not know, they are few
Yet 'round you, surmount you.
Where do you run from trouble?
What you have is a mixed-double
Hope for despair
And round to square
One!
Where do you run?

SWEET LITTLE DAY

December 28, 2012

Looking at the sun, rising
Fumes in the cold winter morning
Jaagi - jaagi dhadkan ke saaz pe machalta
Kaarwaan buland meri neend se guzarta
जागी- जागी धड़कन के साज़ पे मचलता
कारवां बुलंद मेरी नींद से गुज़रता
Mehke- mehke foolon ki khushbu mein ghulta
Raat ki pagdandiyon se raasta nikalta
महके-महके फूलों की ख़ुशबू में घुलता
रात की पगडंडियों से रास्ता निकलता
O sweet little day,
I remember waking up to you!
O sweet little day!
Wide open arms, calling
Field, family, fans following
Khatte- meethe rishton ki chaah mein badhta
Tera- mera karke bhi sang- sang chalta
खट्टे- मीठे रिश्तों की चाह में बढ़ता
तेरा- मेरा करके भी संग-संग चलता
Badli- badli zindagi mein roz hai dhalta
Koi naya mausam, to koi rang kal ka

बदली- बदली ज़िंदगी में रोज़ है ढलता
कोई नया मौसम, तो कोई रंग कल का
O sweet little day!
I remember waking up to you!
O sweet little day!

PICTURES

December 27, 2012

I see you flipping pages,
Of emotion with time.
They are peeping from cages
Of captured bright light
You grab and behold
They fall right in place
A corner in the heart or
A smile on your face.
Pictures, they dwell in our eyes
And I'm dumb in delight,
I see them alive!
You put them in sight
Shapes, sizes and frames
You see them day 'n' night
Like people with names.
They are out in the street
Like a stray thought chain
Branding a fleet
Of pocketed gain.
Pictures, they dwell in our eyes
And I'm dumb in delight,
I see them alive!
You click good and bad

You click people and place
You make happy sad
And you make it with grace.
They talk in and out
In relative disguise
When lonesome they shout
In assembly, abide.
Pictures, they dwell in our eyes
And I'm dumb in delight
I see them alive!

WHAT ARE WE AS A NATION?

December 20, 2012

What are We as a nation?
The proud percentages of vote banks
The physical fist-cuffs in parliament.
One fair man against a corrupt ten
Dilwalon ki dilli, the gang-rape-men.
Some wait for salvation
Others make for celebration
What are We as a nation?
Gold medals, Olympic achievement
To the electoral embarrassment…
Swadeshi, the economic movement
To FDI, a brand attunement,
Foreign language, in national conversation
Foreigners, leading administration
What are We as a nation?
Feeding souls by the pavement
Wombs lost in merriment,
Tax-paying public servant
Fraud scams by government,
Some clean plates, search ration
Others sweep their portion
What are We as a nation?
Telangana procurement

To Kaveri water vent,
Honour killing clans
Naxalite militants.
Some breathe pollution
While others intoxication
So what are We as a nation?

WELCOME TO LIFE

December 19, 2012

Welcome to the paraphernalia of life
Drowning in the sands of time unbound
Crossing one half of the hourglass to another…
And now that you have, come along
And watch the dance of
Simplistic issues of gravity and more,
Of being with, and of and for the materials
Which you never gain, nor lose
Just grow over with and move on.
Welcome to the greatest joys of lives
Of dying men living upon your supplies
And the resurrection of true delight…
…and finally welcome, to the goodbyes
To leaving it all behind
For another to catch, and then let fall!

REACH FOR THE STARS

December 19, 2012

Barren lands of expectations
Never saw no rain, no gain, no pain.
Raising hands in supplication
Found little charm to claim a grain.
Traversing miles of celebration,
Gasping for breath, in the last homebound train.
Kabhi milo to batayein
Kitne badale tohre bin
Pehle har mausam ek din tha
Ab mausam saare hi ek din.
कभी मिलो तो बतायें
कितने बदले तोहरे बिन
पहले हर मौसम एक दिन था
अब मौसम सारे ही एक दिन
Baat guzar kah jaati thi
Meri saari hawaon ko
Jaane thaam kyun na paati thi
Vo apne paanvon ko,
बात गुज़र कह जाती थी
मेरी सारी हवाओं को
जाने थाम क्यूं ना पाती थी

वो अपने पाँवों को

Ab aasmaan kinaare ka

Sir choom raha hoon

Main taaron sang hoon

Ghoom - jhoom raha hoon.

अब आसमान किनारे का

सिर चूम रहा हूँ

मैं तारों संग हूँ

घूम-झूम रहा हूँ

I'm reaching for the stars

They are shining bright

Oh what a delight

I'm reaching for the stars.

I ASKED FOR YOU

December 13, 2012

Yesterday, as I went to bed
I asked for someone to hold me
I asked for a kiss on my forehead
And for eyes to watch me sleep.
I asked for you!
Beyond the curtains upon my window
Behind the shadows of trees
There peeped a twig in clearance
With moonlight dancing in glee.
I asked for you!
The night glimmered darker
And the cold winds biting
I asked for a warm rug
To cover me in hiding.
I asked for you!
And when my eyes closed
In a moment of sleep and trance
I asked for a dream to bury me
In its world of buoyance.
I asked for you!

AND LIFE BEGAN

December 12, 2012

It was always myself, I was looking for none
The race dissolved, and life began.
From dreams to belief
From pain to relief
Life yearning to dare
Life gasping for air
Apnaa dard chhudaye yahan sab, kaun ise samjhaye
Kaun ise samjhaye ki *apnaa dard naa chhooda jaye*
Bachpan ki ummeed se lekar jeevan ki manjhdaar tak
Sab hi gote khayen yahan ab, kaun ise samjhaye
अपना दर्द छुड़ाए यहाँ सब, कौन इसे समझाए
कौन इसे समझाए कि अपना दर्द ना छोड़ा जाए
बचपन की उम्मीद से लेकर जीवन की मँझधार तक
सब ही गोते खायें यहाँ अब, कौन इसे समझाए
The race dissolved
And life began (background).
In the cacophony of the crowd
shout!
In the distilled image of truth
doubt!
In the heinous crimes of house
proud!
Apnaa dard chhudaye yahan sab, kaun ise samjhaye

Kaun ise samjhaye ki *apnaa dard naa chhooda jaye*
Pyaar ke pahle khat se lekar aakhri darkaar tak
Man ko ekal paayen yahan sab, kaun ise samjhaye
अपना दर्द छुड़ाए यहाँ सब, कौन इसे समझाए
कौन इसे समझाए कि अपना दर्द ना छोड़ा जाए
प्यार के पहले ख़त से लेकर आखिरी दरकार तक
मन को एकल पाएँ यहाँ सब, कौन इसे समझाए
The race dissolved
And life began (background).
The dilemma decides
Journey of minds
Living across choice
In the head's voice
Apnaa dard chhudaye yahan sab, kaun ise samjhaye
Kaun ise samjhaye ki *apnaa dard naa chhooda jaye.*
अपना दर्द छुड़ाए यहाँ सब, कौन इसे समझाए
कौन इसे समझाए कि अपना दर्द ना छोड़ा जाए
The race dissolved
And life began (background).

LITTLE LOVE

December 10, 2012

They cross our roads
And cross our minds
They cross every junction in space and time.
They are living out of hope
Out of roof and rain
They are living out of the dirty drain.
Little love to share,
Little hope to dare
Little life to live in despair
Oh! Little human affair!
At the break of dawn our smiles
Reflected in our happy lives
Step out of their comfortable homes.
They are there by the road
By the side of our lives
Parallel, yet in opposite stride.
Little love to share,
Little hope to dare
Little life to live in despair
Oh! Little human affair!
Let each day be given,
And none be left to receive.
Let life be a simple joy,

And simple be its needs.
Hefty loads shared,
For the uphill road to tread.
Broader smiles leading
The grief's to retreat.
Little love to share,
Little hope to dare
Little life to live in despair
Oh! Little human affair!

CHANGING PARADIGM

December 6, 2012

They have told him to refrain
Revealing his identity
They know well to judge and tell
That he's not what they want him to be.
They are never shy from peeping
Into the contours of his daily life
And yet, they never see themselves
Reflected in his ebbs and highs.
Whenever he could prove a change
In himself to his own belief
He was told by them again that
He was only his parody!
They changed his name to this and that
And never could they spell it right
They marked him in his territory
As an animal with no insight.
He has travelled far and yonder
In distant thought and racing time
To exemplify his life at peace
With their changing paradigm.

DEEP IN THE CORNER OF MY ASHTRAY

November 28, 2012

Holding life hand in hand, I just carried on my way
Crafting each worry, deep in the corner of my ashtray
Setting fire to the residual desire, deep in the corner of my ashtray
Gathering crumbs of hope entire, deep in the corner of my ashtray.
Somebody told me it all goes vain
If you cast your days in pain
So here I am casting it all away
Deep in the corner of my ashtray.
Found life as one finds Fate
Cupid, mystic, magic, hate
But I'm searching for none today
Deep in that corner of my ashtray.
Setting fire to the residual desire, deep in the corner of my ashtray
Gathering crumbs of hope entire, deep in the corner of my ashtray
Where the grieved meet the happy, and the fresh meets the frayed
Crossing midnight to midday, deep in the corner of my ashtray.

So much white light in the day, so much black to sweep away
It all burns down to grey, deep in the corner of my ashtray.
Setting fire to the residual desire, deep in the corner of my ashtray
Gathering crumbs of hope entire, deep in the corner of my ashtray.

LET'S

November 22, 2012

Let's pursue gloom, I said
Let's never be happy again,
And detest all that is to be loved
And love the insane.
Let's sow the seeds
Of hate and pain
Let's feed the greed
And be profane.
Let's be the clouds,
Dark inside out
And reign upon humanity
Drench it to sprout.
But wait! We have been there, done that
And now we crop the land
Only to find an alien
In each other's errand.
We ran, we hid
We chained, we died
We buried our souls
And claimed our lives.
We moved away
And never looked back
To realize what

We messed up at.
We fought with the self
And fellow breed
Fought for land, water,
Color and creed.
So let's let go
What we hold so dear
Let's march past
The frontier.
Let the game be played
Now upside down
Let us enjoy loss
As we enjoy the crown.
Let us laugh over
Oneself loud
And let us all differences
Surmount.
Let's lead our way
And live our lives
Let us count our blessings
In disguise!

HYPNO

October 31, 2012

Intriguing labels, wine and rum
Life's been a conundrum.
Dark eyes, darker view;
Loud smiles, louder hue.
Creative entropy of sound,
Amazing enigma all around.
Let the letters flow! The magic glow! And let no logic capture
The sneaking beauty of a mountain peak! And let the music rise and fall!!
Rise and fall!!
Drown and dive in all!!

LIVING IN THE HEAD!

October 6, 2012

We live more in our heads,
don't we?
The simple act of trying
to get a paper plane flying,
Can mean a step towards the moon to one
or just waste of time to someone!
We live more in our heads,
we all do!

A BREATHING PAUSE

September 21, 2012

It settles for a holy cause;
Like the stars fade away at sight.
Life runs on a breathing pause-
'the addictive sadness of falling flight'.
Like the stars that fade away at sight,
One can't count the blessings in disguise.
The addictive sadness of falling flight,
and limitation of the sacred skies.
One can't count the blessings in disguise
And hence the humble retreat to despair,
With limitation of the sacred skies
which no true horizon can declare.
And hence the humble retreat to despair,
It settles for a holy cause.
Where no true horizon shall declare
and life runs on a breathing pause.

TRANQUIL TRAIL

September 1, 2012

Can it be pursued
or does it always need be found?
Does one visit all
Or does it lie within, without?
Is liberation a state of being
or just a state of mind?
How does one comprehend
How does one decide?
It doesn't seem like a beginning
'cause I think I've been here before.
But so is it not a coming back
It makes no sense at all.
Alive awake apprised,
drops of tingling thoughts.
It is a karmic delight
And drenched, my destined lot.

(Just some thoughts penned down on my way back from a serene place!)

NOISES IN MY HEAD

August 28, 2012

Clamouring present
And a silent truth
Kahoon kya wo baat
Jo naa jaanun main.
कहूँ क्या वो बात
जो ना जानूँ मैं
Living real
My nominal identity
Banayee kisne
Meri tasveer esee.
बनायी किसने
मेरी तस्वीर ऐसी
Now that I'm awake
I don't know what to dream!
Abjo payee aankhen
Bin sapne sab rangeen
Ye kahaan ho aayee main
Kaise khud ko sun payee main
Kaise kah dala wo sab
Naa jo khud samajh payee main.
अब जो पायी आँखें,
बिन सपने सब रंगीन
ये कहाँ हो आई मैं

कैसे खुद को सुन पायी मैं
कैसे कह डाला वो सब
ना जो ख़ुद समझ पायी मैं
How do I make it make some sense
I have no clue!
Factual noises
Basic truth.

STORY OF A HOPE

August 17, 2012

Along the sunset line at coast,
there lived by itself, a hope.
It was calm, it was grey
it was all it could ask and pray.
And as all stories preach,
it had somewhere, to reach.
One night, the plot begins
it craved for more.
Crossing its own borders,
it asked for a brighter shore.
It was heavy, the ocean breeze
and hope was too shy to wake her friend.
It flew away in the midsummer sun,
no goodbyes to the sorry end.
It travelled the world and around,
and no body would find it cool.
Changing names and the makeovers
led it to turn into one social fool.
And as they all succumb to flight
it was high on autonomous delight.
It was ambitious, and freed
it was even christened greed!
Identity crisis loomed ahead

and long gone was the willful thrill.
It was tired of feeding its
own self to this everyday drill.
Then came the moment
of climax, martial sad.
It strangled its own desire
and laid it on the death bed.
In the vicinity of such gloom
there was always a silver lining.
And hence hope found,
its long lost repose recline!

NIGHT'S FURY

August 16, 2012

Hey simple gravity,
let me fall
my digital ether
clings after all!
I'm running up and down
the memory lane
and look what I've found,
it's a board game!
Move two blocks
and I am dead
or save some time
'coz it's in my head.
My chattering mind
now talks aloud.
to whom I know not,
is that a doubt?
O dear night!
stop playing this record,
where I am the slave
and you are my lord.
Things turn upside down,
I have no clue
I end up feeling colors,

red, green…BLUE!
So gimme some time
to sing and sigh
and then may I have your
permission to die!
Hey simple gravity
let me fall
my digital ether
clings after all!

ONCE AGAIN

August 5, 2012

Once again in unison
the temple bell shall chime,
we depart, to meet
in yet another time.
Clauses as life puts on you,
you see causes of divide
but as you meet once again,
life knocks again on time...
Once again!
Blooming, grinning and shining,
It's a rock of diamond found,
As you cross a few more tides,
You realize how the world is round..
Once again!
Crossing my mind,
leave back some signs,
I'll follow and meet the Divine
once again!

QUESTIONS

July 24, 2012

Isn't it all about the journey, is that not to gain?
Does it end when we reach, or start when in pain?
Does life go waste, when I seek no definite confusion?
Is the end a beginning to one, or is it a conclusion?
'Why' is never a question, so is not a 'when'
But how does it lead to all, which is being given?
The less I believe, the more I challenge and react.
O creator of justice! My ignorance seeks intellect.

I SHALL CALL FOR YOU

April 11, 2012

When lights drop on a moonless night
When silent thunders no more strike
And the gush of lost wind blows away
The sky's seamless canopy
I shall call for you.
When no sound can penetrate
The wisdom of an illiterate
No writing can be read out loud
Nor good reason be allowed
I shall call for you.
When crumbles down the blimey God
No one can find peace or abode
No praise nor mercy fumigate
And I can no more alliterate
I shall call for you.

AND I SAID TO MYSELF

April 9, 2012

"Why don't you start with telling a story?
Create an environment that breathes of love,
Of childhood dreams and sunrise's glory
And waters as deep as skies above?"
Jo sune na barson se, bachpan ke meethe geet
Aao tum bhi baant lo mere man ka yah sangeet.
Ek adhuri raag hai, par poori hai yah preet
Jaan loge gar milo saavan ke bichhude meet.
जो सुने ना बरसों से, बचपन के मीठे गीत
आओ तुम भी बाँट लो मेरे मन का ये संगीत
एक अधूरी राग है, पर पूरी है ये प्रीत
जान लोगे गर मिलो सावन के बिछड़े मीत
"O', the rain-drenched roof and slippery moonlit sky!"
Ek nazar se dekh lo, ye mausam fir naa aye.
एक नज़र से देख लो, ये मौसम फिर ना आये
"Old cassettes of life,
Playing non-stop melodies,
Lost nothing, gained
True…so true stories!!"
Mohalle kic hhat se guzri hawoan ka mail
Shaam ki batti hai bujhti, raat ka yah khel.
Ek tooti raushni sa jalta tha vo tail
Dhun sunane aa rahi ek door jaati rail.

मौहल्ले की छत से गुज़री हवाओं का मेल
शाम की बत्ती है बुझती, रात का ये खेल
एक टूटी रौशनी सा जलता था वो तेल
धुन सुनाने आ रही एक दूर जाती रेल

So,

"Why don't you start with telling a story?
Create an environment that breathes of love,
Of childhood dreams and sunrise's glory
And waters as deep as skies above?"

THE PSYCHOLOGY OF TRUTH

January 15, 2012

I love myself the most
but still sometimes I lie.
Most of it is fake I know
but I never let me find…why…
Broken shadows if they were
I'd fix them in my head and count
One it is and shall always be
yet I don't see the point I found.
No matter how real it feels to be
I reconstruct a world or two
Where all of it is a jeopardy
and life is minus all I could do…
They tell me I do it all the time
I know they know and hence they do
And I don't know which side of a dime
is my way-win and my way-lose.
Yet every time I happen to cross
this fake line of truth and dare,
I like the sound it makes to toss
Yet not lose the game unfair!

ON THE MEDIAN OF LIFE

October 5, 2011

Gazing into a far thought
or into a thoughtless trace,
I often move between the lines
and read above the space.
A third eye to my charm
a fictional being at view,
I look at myself and all around
as if I were just you.
Bird's eye to all chaos
and constant beep of peace,
Reaching the farthest point of existence
and I cease to be just me.
No clutter to hold back my flight,
and no fear of falling through,
Unseen dream of the lost world
coming to life all anew.
And in all this cognizance, breaks,
the facade of my truth,
I sensitise to the world above,
beneath, within and through.

Thereafter, I wonder how
we make all attempts to strife,
The very essence of being there
on the median of life.

YOU FIND ME!

February 26, 2011

You find me
every now and then,
not confronting myself
running away from you.
You find me
in the vicinity
of hope and delight,
sublime – out of consciousness.
You find me
believing in you
yet never letting me trust
my own mirage of truth.
You find me
finding myself
through you.
Oh me! You've found out, haven't you!

MERELY ALIVE

February 21, 2011

I hurried down the lane
Grabbing my only dream
That someday I shall hear
The requiem for my scream.
Shouting incessantly I ran,
Proclaiming the desire to win.
But never did die my hunger
Nor did that sin.
I thought I had lost and found
And had lost yet again the will,
'cause time was slipping beneath the
Sheets of temporary uphill.
No tragic end to dreams
And no simmering regret,
Yet anguish turned me to ashes
And made life a bet.
Every breath was cheating
On every second's suicide.
The last few moments I lived
Were the last ones I died.

WORLD OF MY OWN MAKING

February 18, 2011

In the conscious wind of turmoil
I let myself sway,
And look up to no one to catch
'cause I like the way it stays.
Though I know it hurts to die
But who can escape fate?
The fate which I create for myself
And the one which makes me create.
A vicious cycle of hope – defeat,
Of tides that rise and fall.
No matter how much you hold to yourself
You are but one after all.
And so am I, in the middle
Of my awakening with Thee,
Of believing that I don't come here to rise
But, to raise the sleeping me.
And hence I plunge into the self,
Into what you have been waking
And leave it all behind except,
The world of my own making.

A DEDICATION TO LATE MRS KALPANA CHAWLA

(The brave journey of a simple idea to time and beyond, through space!)

In the journey of life
it counts…to travel.
One can never be sure
and yet (can) decide…to travel.
People travel distances
people travel with grace.
Some travel deep down within
some travel into open space.
They all do it their way
that makes them move…they travel.
Though it's tough to accept
but I travel…you travel.
People travel boundaries
people travel faith.
Some travel for a lifetime
and some only a phase.
One announces his plan
one silently decides…to travel.

We might walk the same steps
but each has his own…to travel.
People travel time
people travel at pace.
Some reach for the stars
and some fight the worldly maze.
So when one travels all the way,
isn't the journey that one takes
that constitutes life?
Not the trophy or the pay
or even moments far away
can carry one man alive.
Live thy moment
live thyself.
Carry Time
travel Space!

LOOK! WHERE WE HAVE COME?

Look! Where we have come?
So far so close.
Within, lies the clarity
Without, remorse.
I know it was never how we look
But where
And coming to life, perspective
And the sanctity, to declare…
Irrefutable crime of justice
Difficult to cope
Rising ashes of forlorn magic
Phantasmagoric hope…
So look! Where we have come?
So far so close.
Within, lies the clarity
Without, remorse…

MY IGNORANCE SEEKS INTELLECT...

Every time, they arise
I ask questions
Seeking no definite confusion
Let it be
Let it be.
Isn't it all about the journey
and not about the gain?
Does it end when we reach
or start when in pain?
I seek no definite confusion
Does life go waste when
Is the end, a beginning to one
Or, is it a conclusion?
'Why', is never a doubt
So is not a 'when'
But how does it lead to all
That is given and remains?
O creator of justice! my
Ignorance seeks intellect
The lesser I believe the
More I question and react
O creator of justice! my
Ignorance seeks intellect…

GIVE ME SOME TIME

Hey, simple gravity
let me fall
my digital ether
clings after all.
I'm running up and down
the memory lane
and look what I've found
it's aboard game.
Move two blocks
and I'm dead
or, save some time
because it's in my head.
My chattering mind
now talks aloud
to whom I know not...
is that a doubt?
O dear night
stop playing this record
where I'm the slave
and you are the lord.
Things turned upside down
I have no clue
I end up feeling colors
red green...BLUE

So give me some time
to sing and sigh
and then I may have your
permission to die?

TIME IS NOBODY

Time is nobody.
If it were, I'd have invited it over
last night
in her life
or maybe not,
maybe it was time
and it came, on its own
no invites…no calls
it was a duty maybe.
I see in their eyes.
I don't know if it's her or her absence
but I see it
it's not a void
it's a fulfilment rather
a reverence
and above all, love.
Those irrefutable events have
shaped it all,
and no brimming tear can
wash it away;
it's not pain, nor guilt
nor agony.
It's one of those feelings when you
know you are suffocated
and you know you cannot help it.

You don't give in
but you don't fight either.
"They Took Her Away,"
was what she told me when
I cried.
And then she added like a
silent tear. "And we cannot
bring her back."
He is trampled,
disoriented.
And he is not looking for peace
it's not a sorry state
no single emotion can imitate him.
When I first saw him tonight
I was overwhelmed by his grace.
He shall never be the same
it's only a matter of time, they say…
(The others…outsiders, who don't)
but I don't see that!
It can never be about time
because time, as I said is nobody…
how can there be a story about
nobody…
No, it's about them…
and they are living it…
living her silent exit!
(Escape/ passing away.)
She had tied them all up…

in her own way
and she is doing it wonderfully
...even now!
She can be felt
resonating in their relationship,
she may not be reflected in
her physical being
but they are...all reflected in
HER!

HYPNOS SONG

Sleep, sleep this night
Let the rain wash your tears
And when you wake up
We will battle all your fears.
Sleep, sleep because
It's the night to reveal
Peel off your wound
Let it dry, let it heal.
Sleep, because your sultry eyes
Amaze the ocean beneath
And it's the tide of Time
And the time of rising heat.
Sleep in your dreams, in your past
In everything that doesn't last
But let your sleep last to believe
That it's not sleep but a world
To live, to breathe.
Sleep, dream, live
And wake up to die again
Sleep, dream, live
And wake up to live again to
Sleep again!

IT'S FROM YOU

All my life
Every moment of purity
All my soul
Every part of eternity
All my dreams
Every image of fantasy
It's from you I derive
I desire
I admire
Your brevity
Your sanctity.
All my thoughts
Every goal of unanimity
Every spell of neutrality
All my blessings
Every share of charity
It's from you I derive
I desire
I admire
Your brevity
Your sanctity.
All my hopes
Every tide of prosperity
All my passions
Every drive to…propensity

All my actions
It's from you I derive
I desire
I admire
Your brevity
Your sanctity.

YOU

There's always something in the way
Always something getting through
It's not me
Is it you?
It's you…
It's all I know
It's you!
I find peace when I'm confused
I find hope when I'm let down
It's not in me
Is it in you?
It's in you!
It's all I know
It's you!

DREAM

Daring, courageous
Heart-throbbing, punching
Regretting, saturating,
Dream.
I dream of you day'n'night,
Within me I find
Not me but just
Your dream.
What is it
That life's gonna snatch away
Through you
How is it
That I'm not gonna get it
That I'm not gonna get you?
Yet I dare
I declare
I claim you, on my own.
Wow…is it just a dream?
A daring dream, daring me to you?
Daring, courageous,
Heart-throbbing, punching
Regretting, saturating
Dream.
I dream of you day-night,
Inside me I find

Not me but just
Your dream.
What is it
That life's gonna snatch away
Through you?
How is it
That I'm not gonna get it
That I'm not gonna get you?
Yet I dare
I declare
I claim you.
Wow…i3s it just a dream?
A daring dream, daring me to you?

LIFE IS A BLISS

There's this ocean of emptiness
I'm filled and
I will drown
In this state. I wasn't
When it had all just begun
But now that it's over
I'm down, smitten...
The consequence, of nothing
But a coincidence
And a coincidence of just
One moment
One feeling, one desire
Of one oneness to aspire.
Nothing's wrong
After all what can be,
When nothing is to last long
Nothing to hold nothing free?
Empty, it was all
Yet it was,
Was it, I doubt
Yet there was something concrete
Or an illusionary dream
To sprout...
Fake delusionary dream
Turns a real nightmare.

I groan
There's this ocean of emptiness
I'm filled and
I will drown.
Dark is not what it is
It's yellow, green, blue
The sun, the bird, the rain
The morning hue and dew anew.
Yet it is all so lovely
So dull so morose
Like it's the end of all worlds
Laid upon the cross.
Salvation is never vindictive
So forgive yourself for the times you cried
Redemption is to believe
That life's free and moves on
No matter how memories are tied.
Fill the emptiness
With love and content
Life is a bliss
Gloom, just a sentiment,
Life is a bliss
Life is a bliss
Gloom, just a sentiment
Life is a bliss
Life is a bliss!

WHEN YOU ARE GONE

When you are gone
Life is…so maroon.
No wake-up calls, mornings sigh
No sweet dreams, though the moon is high.
Yet I feel you
In the warmth of the sun
I see you in
In the flowing streams.
You are gleaming
In those moonlit nights
And lighting up
The darkness of life.
When you are gone
Life is…so maroon
No wake-up calls, mornings sigh
No sweet dreams, though the moon is high
No wonder it's all over now
But it'll always go on so
This way
You are there in what I do
What I feel what I say.

When you are gone
Life is…so maroon
No wake-up calls, mornings sigh
No sweet dreams, though the moon is high.

IMMORTAL DREAMS

Immortal dreams
don't survive,
when they loot away your sleep.
Vehemently they remain
in your eyes,
take shape
as you are close to the world;
want to
stand by every word
though bizarre,
they belong to me
and they make me what I am
desirous, yet free.
These immortal dreams
I trust, I hold
because they loot away my sleep
to tell, stories untold
waiting to uphold!

FORGET ME NOT

Forget me not, me not
Me not, forget me not
Remember this hot, chilli hot
Chilli hot, forget me not!
I want to swing, I want to swing in this giant world fair
I want to be and only me in this world fair
I want to share with this world that I am not only a girl
Forget me not, me not, me not, forget me not!
I want to say a few words to you dear
I want to be an open book which is clear
I want to be so tempered, so hot
Forget me not, me not, me not, forget me no…t!

(Written on 12 April 2002, at the age of 12)

I HAVE TO LOVE NATURE

To flow in the wind,
to have a mind kind,
I have to love nature.
To create a sound
to turn the world round
I have to love nature.
To come near you
to ask who are you
I have to love nature.
To sleep a long time
to commit a crime
I have to go through nature.

(Written on 13 April 2002, at the age of 12)

TROPHIES OF LIFE

Snatching away the snaps of time
I behold every sublime
Sublime of delight, to mourning sites
Sublime of expression, to smothered nights
I perceive the sultry water, like my eyes.
I can't point to my life's griefs
For life's distressed naught.
I can't stop for life makes
Only a single halt,
I need to move,
I need to face with grace,
I need to bear every phase,
I need to carry on the race.

LIFE'S BRIEF GRIEF

A time will come when I'll
Get the best of this life
Life's every moment would be mine
And I will be of every time.
I'll glide in the clouds
With dreams steadfast
I'll never fail to try
My luck on…
And the world will share
My exuberant talent
And have no sign in life
Of disgust or lament.

LEAVING BEHIND

Leaving behind
Every site of passing coffer
Walk forth
Move ahead
And begin a new life.
Live in memories
But don't cling to them
For Time is finite
You need to move
With less load
By your side.
Phases come
When faces fade
Into your eyes
What's in your heart is
The real picture
Of your sight.
Life never stops
Time never waits
Nor ever should we then take a break
Always remember
It's life and not a game
And each passing day is never the same.

CANADA

IN THE VICINITY OF HOPE

In the vicinity of hope
lies a real me, a real you
a real world,
to cope.
We can always be together
as this journey goes on,
but life has different rules
for all who come along.
So, no matter there's hope
there'll always be scope,
because theirs, is this real world
to cope.
...
Far beyond me, I stay
away from this world
where life's yet to begin
lies a beautiful world.
In the vicinity of the woods
I try to cope with the falls
not that it's done when said
but when said came no calls.

Hopes, they die
words, they fade
lasts is what
I tend to…

THE ROAD TO TIME

The road to Time
Has always been rocky, deserted
Catching up with things
Gone and yet to arrive
I always fail to drop
Fail to derive
It's the road to Time
I touch it, and touch the sublime.
Never turning back
No way to escape
Every step, crossroads
Every road, different stakes
It's the road to Time
I touch it, and touch the sublime.

I AM NOWHERE

Every time in unanimity
there's spontaneity.
I fight it
I defy it
I reject it
I object to it.
It's not love, it's not care
it'll never be hope, always despair.
Because it's you, you only are there
I'm gone, I'm nowhere,
I'm nowhere, nowhere.
Every time in your vicinity
there's this lone activity
I feel it
I conceal it
I criticize it
I oblige it.
It's not courage, it's not dare,
it'll always be tough to compare.
Because it's you, you only are there
I'm gone, I'm nowhere,
I'm nowhere, nowhere.

ADAMANT IN THEIR SPEECH

Unambiguous lies,
adamant in their speech.
A lore to human ties
A bang of social breach
lies to truth, satire
lumps of dump, desire
preserved in their minds.
Unambiguous lies
adamant in their speech.
Consoling for deeds of own creation
counting attainable goals, mere anticipation
it's not what is intended
but what is to be preached.
Unambiguous lies
adamant in their speech.
Shattered are the ones with faith
culprits to humanity, celebrate,
it's not their end that will end it
but it's core their crime should be seized.
Unambiguous lies
adamant in their speech.
Stories of uniqueness, they aspire
but fame and riches expire

life is a journey
not a destination to reach.
Unambiguous lies
adamant in their speech.

THE INCARNATION OF TRUTH

Sometimes, to just permeate events
And to rationalize thoughts over deeds
Truth takes vulnerable turns
To make the world believe, pay heed.
Succumb to death, lies entailed
And times go by worn out
Truth is not legitimate these days
But its cousins sprout.
Not that time is changing
Nor is the world to blame
It's the incarnation of truth
Born of corruption, ill-fame.

PARODY OF LIFE

It's just a parody of life to lose
But the melody is to choose.
So let the renaissance of joy
Every drop of color you employ
Watch out, for the mountain peaks that sublime
Hit it, it's the temple bell that chimes
See the morning dews, dazzling the sunshine
And the lovely evening hues, so benign.
It was downhill that you fell, don't lag
Catch up fast, come-on, drag
So hold on to the presence of those near
They are diamonds, forever dear
Let them touch the banks, embrace
Leaving footsteps, you may trace.
Admire it, this is life all gains
Only memories, no trance, no pains.
So choose your way out
Choose your way in
Let it go, trying
Let it begin.
Let it hurt, let it cry
Let it grow, let it try
Let it boil, let it fry

Just let it live, let it fly
Let them in and glow
Feel it and let it flow
Let be with them, let them be
Just sail all your boats, set free
Set it free!

IN ME YOU FLOW

When in the sunbeams you pass
deliberately through my thoughts, you surprise me.
Singing to me the greatest symphony of life,
you declare somehow that you like me.
All emotions on fire
each moment, a desire…
You surprise me
and that's all I know
in me you, in you I flow.

A DREAM...I AM LIVING

In the silence of the roars of the day
And in the nights' screaming, scorching monotony
I glare up at the skies
And close my eyes
And I close my eyes
My eyes, your eyes.
I plunge into
Your dreams I bear, I see
You see
We see…the dream.
Is it fake?
Is it not…or is it just a dream
A dream… I am living
Living?
Living or not?
Is it blue
Or black?
Or it's just grey
I'm plunging into…?
It's there but….
Is it?
Or it's not…
What a question…is this…life…
Is it a question?
Or a solution?

It's something...
Say yes
No...
Is it not?...?...?
Confused... I am
As I have always been
Not very keen
But confused
I am
Am I?
Or am not?...?...?
Surviving the depleting energy of my life
You stand there alone
Me alone
We alone
And don't know how...
No more alone
Yet alone
We survive...
Up in the skies
The moon is bright
It's a full moon night
No star(s), no clouds
No nothing, but, the moon
Sun to moon(noon)
Rhythm to tune
Yet...alone
The moon

The tune
You to me
Me to you
Yet alone
We stand
Alone
Alone…
What crap was that
This isn't me… No…not me
Now taste my flavour
Fried deep in my stare… NOW!
Higher, higher, higher, higher, higher
Higher I fly, fly, fly, fly
Higher I reach
The more I see, see, see
The more I believe
You are true
Like these birds flying with me
You are true
Like the sunny heat I feel
You are true
Like the cloudy winds that blow
You are true
Like the mighty moon's glow
And it's no dream
Because in flying (flying, flying)
Flying high, high, high
I'm higher, higher, higher

High in the sky
I'm flying high in the skies with you, you, you.
------ Sound of drums -------
Hold me tight
We are in flight
In the dusty rusty
Road to life
Road to live
We still
We do not pass the fun on the ride
So we are
Flying high
Flying in the skies yeah! High!

SOMEWHAT?

Somewhat unidentified
look on your face
Somewhat I know
that not all is right
Somewhat I try
to guess what's wrong
Somewhat you pause to
say you are strong
Somewhat…somewhat
we share
Somewhat…somewhat
we hide
Somewhat…somewhat
we live
Somewhat…somewhat
it's you and I
Somewhat…somewhat…somewhat
Somewhat…somewhat…somewhat
Somewhat…somewhat…somewhat…
Hey! Let's make this somewhat
disappear altogether
Let it all be clear
in sunny cloudy weather
Let us not reason
let us not try

Because all I know is
all is not right
So…
this is all I wish
that's all I hope
that something is not
but something is to cope
Hey!…that's all…
Hey!…that's all!

ONLY FOR YOU

You can't march ahead
Without any passion
Just must carry on
With a force of action.
Pray to the divine
After every good deed
For a bright sky
You are just a seed.
Infusing in you
The glare of gallant
Revitalizing your
Latent talent.
You are the brightest
In the firmament
In your power
Adamant.
This
You can do
For it's
Only for you.

PLIGHT OF THE EARLIEST BIRD

I need space to die
The land may not suffice
I need the whole sky
I am the early bird in flight.
I was the first to be served by dawn
I was the first to be born on my own
But I wasn't the first to bright
I am the early bird of night.
I am the one who chirped in your tree
As the night gathered, bid goodnight with glee
But I wasn't the first to sight
I am the earliest bird in plight.

MY MOTHER'S WAYS

She makes me cry
And brings on smiles
By staying back
Or walking miles
Puts on my courage
Gears up for the day
That's how I feel
Is my mother's way.
She settles everything so well
And calms the rising seas
As rough as though
The tide may be
Always on time is she
And turns on the passive
To willful happiness
That's why I praise
My mother's ways.

CELEBRATED KNIGHTS

The tapestries over human life
Have grown out of gloomy nights
Remote faces, demonizing lights
This is the story of celebrated knights.
Charioteered by harassing media
Dragged by mercenary crowds
Bound to live, confined to death
Yet in odd times, they sprout.
Which souls have they
To survive thus long?
To the heaven of God
Did they belong?
As the time that
They never abhor
So shall we then
Them adore.

(14 Nov. 2005.This poem was written against the backdrop of the death of Princess Diana. Paparazzi pursued her vehicle, resulting in her untimely death.)

THE MURLI TALES

Along the Ganges
It flew as a blare
The thrashing water flow
They drew it in flare
And passersby can never
Forget those mystic mails
Still enchanting the valley
Are the Murli Tales.
From the patrons of Time
To the superstitious regime
No soul was left untouched
By Murli's mimes.
But the magic can no longer last
As the mind flickers so fast
I can't recall what I believe
A dream of the distant past?

CALL FOR PEACE

The breathing silence
Its roars unheard
Whirls withered
With peace of losing tempers
The fate of good old duty
Its signs all tattered
Come home, return
Oh! Mercy
By your bliss
We are all sheltered.
Live, come to life
Bring smiles
Of prayerful delight
To each dying soul
Nourish their lofty goals
With the power of your benign presence
To add to their life's essence.

MAZES

Tracking tranquility
Serenading smiles
The world a maze
In amazing styles.
Born of new days
Worn of old stuffs
Treading to make
Some mesmerizing bluffs.
Aiming infinity
Running miles
Leading a race
Of lost tribes.
Call of echoes, awake
Their sounds more of mites
Buzzing each day
Dreading scorpion bites.
Rating up
The human sides
Growing in
The snobby streets
Mazes create
Mazes destroy
The life of every humble retreat.

ONCE AGAIN-1

Once again
Life has turned around
As we return home
Trying to make of life
What we really want.
This is life
Simply moving on
Packing the times
Spent and gone.
Gone to create
Some new space
With new friends
At some new place.
So here, once again
We depart
To start
another life
With a promise to keep
That we depart to meet
Another time…
Snatching away the snaps of Time
I will behold this sublime

Treading towards the goals
Leave back some signs
I will follow and meet the Divine
Once again.

ONCE AGAIN-2

Once again in unison
I am in one more time
We depart, to meet
Another time.
Clauses as life puts on you
You see, causes of divide
But when you meet again
Life knocks back on Time
Once again.
Blooming, grinning, shining
It's a diamond rock found
As you cross a few more tides
You realize how the world is round
Once again.
Snatching away the snaps of Time
I will behold this sublime
Treading towards the goals
Leave back some signs
I will follow and meet the Divine
Once again.

THOSE LITTLE THINGS

The little things I did not do
The little things I did wrong to you
The little things I hid from you
Those little things bit you.
I remember walking in my dreams by your side
I remember being close to you somewhere, sometime
I don't know how much it hurts
But never will it be whole, I apologize.
My mornings all saw your face or died
My noon was all your smiling insight
My evenings though crazy and bizarre
With you they always lit up, though I lied.
So here you know it's all me or mine
Now here I see you crossing my line
Like I always knew I was evil to you
You loved me with a heart so fragile.
I say kill me, save me, from this pain
No love, no life, no gain remain
It's always easy to shine in the sun
Then to melt away in pouring rain.

I HAVE A SONG

I have a song,
a voice to tap my soul.
I have a song,
some words to buoy my spirit.
I have a song,
a rhythm my heart beats to.
I have a song,
a symphony of thousands of bleeding nephrons.
I sing along
with nature – a spirited deer
into the woods, around the brooks…
I have a song!

LOOK DEEP BEFORE YOU DIE

Behind the facade of your eye
look deep before you die.
They might save a day or two
because they know your real I.
Seek a chance to peer through
a little, in the dark of your side.
The far may seem closer
and close would go for a ride.
Shallow inside out, nowhere
will you find it right.
Until it's dark and gloomy
and no sight all night.
Unborn terrors of the grave
visiting every birth of joy
Don't you hide enough to know
they have broken all your toys?
Live the fear, live the cry
live till you can no more try.
And then live just one more day
before you leave this world and fly.

HEAL ME

Mend me O Lord,
heal me and all my wounds
heal my mind
because it's empty and full
empty…of you
Full…of me
heal me.
Heal my soul
because it's found and stolen
found in me
stolen from you
heal me.
Heal my body
because it's empty and full
empty…of you
full…of me
heal me.
Heal my heart
because it's one and broken
broken in me,

yet one in you
heal me…
heal me…
heal me.

SHOULD I THANK YOU?

Sometimes I gaze at you
In your eyes, I meet myself
Yet keep gazing back
No charm no twinkles
No sultry viciousness
Pure unadulterated truth…
I see a deep blank sea
I dive and drown
You catch me sometimes
And some other times…
I smile.
You don't know that you don't know
And I let you…
Again I smile
It's a rainy day
And they let me rain…
I don't smile
No more
I gaze at you though…
You know what I mean!
Should I thank you?

BEAUTIFUL NIGHT?

Oh! Beautiful night!
With all your stars and moon in delight
Moon the bridegroom and moonlight the bride
Stars tired but standing in pride
Oh! How beautiful, the night!
Sky singing with joy
Sun playing with toy
In his bedroom wearing a night-dress light
Oh! How beautiful, the night!
Moon and his wife are paired
But everyone is scared
As, this all will be carried away by morning tide
Oh! How beautiful, the night!

THE WRONG WORLD

The sunset rising
The sunrise setting
The earth gives light
The sun gives life
The father is giving birth
The mother is going to work
The students telling
The teachers listening
The school is having sports
The playground is having classes
The thief is having his station
The police in prison
The servant is ordering tea
The master preparing it with glee
Sandals made of gold
Jewelry made of leather
The oceans overflowing with milk
Babies are drinking water
Sheep are clad in sweaters
The skin of man is wool

How wonderful it would be
If world would turn wrong
With Shiva is bathing in roti
And man bathing in milk.

Make Me Fly

Like a star which shines in my sky
every night
Like a hand in all my sweats
holds on tight
Like the first rain, calming, soothing
brings delight…
And makes me - all right!
You make me sing
make me dance
make me fly.
You make me love myself
reach thyself
make me try!
All right!
Mending my life
healing my cries
weaving my relations
breaking my dawn
cutting through clutched yawns
you root away all frustrations.

HAVE A 'FALL'

Thoughts
dwindling rise and
a fall
a deep fall.
Caressing smiles
who knows
they have a truth
but they are false
and a fall.
Hopes
sustaining lives
may be shallow
but
have a great force
to make a fall
a deep fall.
Those
who really care
don't deserve
this rise of fall
but who cares
go 'have a "Fall".'

O WHAT LIGHT

Slow agreement
of winter with sunshine
and hazy shadows
cross my sight.
Oh! What a day to start afresh,
to start a season of dreams
where no limits are boundaries
and no hope is lost in mist.
What a day!!
Whole night awake
I think of sunrise
and as I drown in sleep
it's daylight.
O what light beaming,
it's facing all my fears
there is no hiding back in time
where no peace ever reclined
O what light!!

GARDEN OF HOPE

When you wake up
we'll battle all your fears.
But for now I'll
hold my heart back,
leave all pictures
on the floor,
take back only
my memories –
I can't take it
Anymore.
In the courtyard of life
tucked away out of sight,
I have a teeny-tiny
garden of hope.

IN THE END

In the end you know
when to just stop the conversation
how to say goodbye
without the things said and done.
In the end you talk
not about us, but of others
of things abstract
of logic and philosophers.
In the end it's usual
yet unusual to believe
that it's not what we see
but what we perceive.
In the end we depart
with no promises to keep
yet expectations to forget
memories frail and deep.
...and in the end
we claim to choose different ways.
Differences move far away
yet we stay.
In the end...